INTRODUCTION

Everyone loves box turtles; everyone. Children, young adults, old adults. Box turtles, and for that matter turtles in general, don't seem to have that terrifying effect on people that snakes and some lizards do. They are slow-moving, long-lived, creatures, then this book is for you. It was written with the aspiring hobbyist in mind. There is a little natural history and taxonomy information thrown in, but only a small amount. The real focus is on how to keep your box turtles alive

L. QUINN.

Box turtles are among the most charming of all turtle pets. They are hardy and very long-lived. Photo of an Eastern Box Turtle, *Terrapene carolina*.

hardy, friendly, clever, and in many cases quite attractive. They respond well to captivity (under the correct conditions, of course) and, once fully adjusted, they will live healthy, happy lives. They are one of the few members of the herpetological world that a keeper could have around for life. Specimens over 100 years old are not unusual. Isn't that fascinating?

If you have an interest in such and well. That is, after all, the main goal. A keeper should take pride in healthy specimens and endeavor to keep them that way. Remember, every creature you keep is solely dependent on you for its well-being. Its life is in your hands. That's why a book like this is so useful—it helps you deal with that task.

Successfully, I hope.

Jordan Patterson

Even for someone interested strictly in the *keeping* of box turtles, a general section on natural history, zoogeography, taxonomy, and so forth can be helpful. Such information gives the enthusiast a better understanding of the animal he or she is housing and studying, and, if that enthusiast is a sharp enough student, they can use such knowledge to better their husbandry techniques and thus improve the lives of their captives, which is of course the constant goal in any facet of herptile keeping.

THE PROBLEM WITH COMMON NAMES

In the hobby of herpetology, the general tendency to use common names rather than scientific ones is very strong. Although there has been a trend of late for keepers to learn the Latin monikers of their animals, the common English classifications still prevail due to the fact that pet stores and breeders will want to be sure their customers are fully aware of what they are seeing and, hopefully, purchasing. In short, just about all interested persons will know what a box turtle is, but not all will know that same animal is also known as *Terrapene ornata*, *Terrapene carolina*, or whatever.

The problem with this, however, is that common names can sometimes be confusing because they are only abstract concepts at best; that is to say they are not "real." For example, many common names are based on things like folklore or the name of the person who either first described the animal or had something similar to do with it. But what does that tell us about the animal itself from a scientific point of view? Not much. Common names are weak and can be too broad whereas scientific names are more specific and exact (or at least they try to be).

The animals we are discussing here are box turtles, but the name "box turtle" is not generally ascribed to one genera of chelonians; it is attributed to two—*Terrapene*, which is the genus most familiar to hobbyists, and *Cuora*, the "Asian box turtles." That would be confusing to almost anyone wouldn't it? If you spoke of box turtles in a broad sense, who would know which genera you are talking about? Members of the genera *Cuora* and *Terrapene* are vastly different in many ways, so speaking of them under the same vernacular can be very misleading.

To solve this problem within the confines of this section of the book, I will discuss the genus *Terrapene* exclusively and restrict attention of *Cuora* to a separate chapter later on (except in the case of the checklist included here, which I wish to present complete). The chapter on disease and so on will still apply to both genera, as will most of the data on acquiring specimens, but beyond that, the Asian Box Turtles will be given a focus all their own.

THE GENUS *TERRAPENE*

Speaking etymologically, the name *Terrapene* assumedly means land turtle, *terra* meaning ground or earth and *terrapen* being a word for turtle.

The name *Terrapene* was first utilized in conjunction with box turtles in 1820 by Merrem. Turtles in this genus were first placed in *Testudo* by Gmelin in 1789, based on Linnaeus in 1758.

The box turtles of this genus are most easily identified by their high-domed shell, stumpy feet (which are not webbed), a carapace with a well-developed median keel, and the ability to close up within their shells completely; a very effective defensive attribute which has undoubtedly saved them from the ravages of many a natural predator.

Most *Terrapene* box turtles are omnivorous, taking basically whatever foods are available. They have been known to show a greater tendency toward meat when younger and then switch off to an almost exclusive fruit and vegetable diet in their later years. This, however, can change during times of extreme

stretches of thick woodland but rarely far from water. They are not particularly good swimmers but will crawl into shallow pools and puddles every now and then to drink or cool off on intolerably hot days. Those of the western and more southerly regions wander around dry prairies and so forth. They too will stay close to reliable water sources. In nonspecific terms, the

DR. HERBERT R. AXELROD.

It is generally believed that the genus name for the North American box turtles, *Terrapene*, means "land turtle." Photo of a Common Box Turtle, *Terrapene carolina*.

circumstance. They have been known to accept a variety of berries, flowers, buds, earthworms, snails, beetles, flies, and even mushrooms.

The natural habitat of the *Terrapene* box turtles varies from place to place. Those in the northeast can be found in quiet

geographical range of this genus includes most of the United States (absent from the western third) and scattered in sections of central and southern Mexico.

THE SPECIES

There are currently four accepted

species in the genus *Terrapene*—*T. carolina* (Common Box Turtle), *T. ornata* (Ornate Box Turtle), *T. nelsoni* (Spotted Box Turtle), and *T. coahuila* (Coahuilan Box Turtle). Since each species has many subtle differences in relation to each other, it would be more sensible to investigate them individually rather than collectively.

COMMON BOX TURTLE
TERRAPENE CAROLINA
(Linnaeus, 1758)

The natural range of this most popular hobby species includes

KEN LUCAS.

There are currently six accepted subspecies of the Common Box Turtle. The one shown here is the Florida Box Turtle, *Terrapene carolina bauri*

most of the eastern United States (getting sparser as it goes north) and sections of eastern Mexico, most notably to Veracruz and the Yucatan Peninsula. There are six currently accepted subspecies, all with slightly varying colors on the same basic design. The skin is generally very dark brown (almost black), with red, yellow, or orange spotting and streaking. Notably, a fairly reliable and easy way to tell the males from the females is by the color of the iris—in the males it is red, in the females it is more yellowish brown.

Terrapene carolina is generally a diurnal species and can be most often found in the early morning or after sudden rains during the hotter parts of the season. I have come across many after heavy rains. In fact, once, as I was in the field actually searching for this species with no luck whatsoever, a sudden shower came down for about fifteen minutes, and after it ceased I found a male and a female within twenty minutes, no more than thirty or so yards apart from each other! It was most remarkable because, as I said, I had found none up until then. If I wanted to describe the situation surrealistically I would say they simply materialized from the soil. A situation such as this is most common during times when the summer heat is almost oppressive, but during the spring and early fall you can find this species at any time of the day. It likes to forage in high grasses, especially near water bodies (I once found one at the edge of a field near an obscured streambed). It is also possible to locate them near brackish water areas as well, although this is not a common occurrence.

Hibernation for *T. carolina* starts around October in the most northern part of its range but can be delayed until November and sometimes even later in the south. In some places, in fact, the species may not even truly hibernate at all. Generally speaking, a Common Box

Turtle will begin its preparations for winter dormancy when its ambient temperature drops below 65°F/18°C and remains that way with regularity. They will hibernate in loose soil, rotting vegetation, in the muddy beds of streams and lakes, under decaying tree stumps, or in burrows. Generally this hibernation period will only last about four months; over five is exceptional. In the more southerly parts of their range the period is of course much shorter. A most interesting note is that more than once *T. carolina* has

because they have ventured too far from their first den, failed to find another, and then the winter frost returned.

ORNATE BOX TURTLE
TERRAPENE ORNATA
(Agassiz, 1857)

Most of the heavily populated communities of this most attractive box turtle species are located in the mid-western United States, although not extended much more north than the boundary line that divides Nebraska and South Dakota. There

R. T. ZAPPALORTI.

The Eastern Box Turtle, *Terrapene carolina carolina*, was, at one time, a fairly abundant animal. Now, due to, among other things, sharp population decline, it is protected over most of its range.

been observed changing its hibernation site during the winter! On warmer days a specimen may leave its current den and seek out another. Unfortunately such actions have also produced dead turtles

are at present two subspecies being recognized.

Like its genus-mate *T. carolina*, the Ornate Box Turtle is a dedicated daytime animal. It will leave its resting den in the early morning and

There are only two subspecies of the Ornate Box Turtle, *Terrapene ornata*. The Desert Box Turtle, *Terrapene ornata luteola*, is shown here.

almost immediately begin foraging for food. It does not bask often but when it does it will usually do so in the early morning hours when the heat from the sun is not too brutal. Then, as midday approaches, the turtle will find cover and remain cool until the heat begins to taper off during the later afternoon. At this time it will then pick up where it left off and search for more food. When the later dusk hours hit and darkness begins to take over the sunlight, the animal will stop its daily activities and prepare for another night's rest.

T. ornata has a very long active season—usually from March to November—although for the first month or so after hibernation they will do very little in the way of feeding and mating. May is the month in which they really seem to come to life, and then the animals will remain active until about mid-October, which is when preparations for hibernation usually begin. By the end of November, most of them are deep underground.

SPOTTED BOX TURTLE
TERRAPENE NELSONI
(Stejneger, 1925)

There are only two subspecies currently listed in this sparsely distributed species, one being named after noted herpetologist Laurence M. Klauber. Spotted Box Turtles can be found in small populations in northwestern Mexico, most notably in Sonora, Sinaloa, and Nayarit.

The species can be most easily recognized by its narrow oval carapace, which is slightly less domed than those of other members of the genus. Also, the animal has a poorly defined medial keel, which puts it even further out of step with other box turtles. It has a dark brown carapace with a light yellow border (growing darker with age) and usually has bright yellow spots. Although many hobbyists consider a concave plastron to be the easy telling sign of a male turtle, in the Spotted Box Turtle it may not be so easy—sometimes it is only vaguely concave at best and thus hardly reliable (although with some of the females it is not only flat, but even slightly convex).

Captives reportedly do well, taking a wide variety of foods and showing great adaptability, but legally they are highly protected and almost never

Note the red eye on this Ornate Box Turtle, *Terrapene ornata*. This means the animal is very probably a male; the females's eyes are usually brown.

R. T. ZAPPALORTI.

The Ornate Box Turtle, *Terrapene ornata*, is considered an animal of the prairies, mostly inhabiting grassy or barren plains in the mid-western United States. Photo by Mella Panzella.

available. There have rarely been captive breedings, but from what little data are available there is apparently a very low egg clutch number, the average being only two or three.

COAHUILAN BOX TURTLE
TERRAPENE COAHUILA
(Schmidt and Owens, 1944)

This is the box turtle with the most restricted range, only being known from within the vicinity of the type locality—Coahuila, Mexico, in the Cuatro Cienegas Valley. Unsurprisingly, there are no subspecies listed at this time.

It is a shame that this animal is so scarce; it is very attractive and supposedly does well in captivity (although it must be kept in an outdoor enclosure with a high ambient temperature). Its carapace is uniformly colored brownish olive and has only remnants of a medial keel. The head, while also bearing this grayish color, also has tinges of gray and occasionally some dark mottling. The upper jaw is strongly hooked.

Most interestingly, *T. coahuila* is considered the only true aquatic North American box turtle. It occurs in shallow slow-moving or still-water bodies with soft muddy bottoms, usually with a heavy degree of vegetation. It has been known to mate during every season and copulation can occur both in and out of the water. The color of the hatchlings is more brilliant and pronounced than the adults, but this will begin to fade not long after they reach adulthood.

The Coahuilan Box Turtle is an opportunistic feeder and will take items both in and out of the water. It spends much of its time in search of meals and will accept fish, worms, crickets, grasshoppers, small mice, lettuce, apples, bananas, and even canned commercial food. There are undoubtedly other items it will accept as well but the point is that it is not a picky eater and thus would make an excellent species in captivity.

T. coahuila seems to be as equally

chapter a listing of all currently accepted species and subspecies of chelonians we refer to in English as "box turtles." This list is based on John Iverson's superb *A Revised Checklist with Distribution Maps of the Turtles of the World*, which is considered one of the central reference books of its kind in

DR. PETER C. H. PRITCHARD.

Containing only two subspecies, the Spotted Box Turtle, *Terrapene nelsoni*, has a limited range and is never seen in the pet trade.

at home in the water as it is on land, and it will spend most of its time in the former. Occasionally a scavenger, it will not think twice before diving into deeper waters, submerging itself completely in the pursuit of food. However, since populations of this species can be remarkably dense, intense competition often results.

CHECKLIST OF SPECIES

For the sake of completeness, I have decided to include in this

herpetology today (and rightly so).

Genus **TERRAPENE**

NORTH AMERICAN BOX TURTLES

***Terrapene carolina*—Common Box Turtle**

—*T. c. carolina*
—*T. c. bauri*
—*T. c. major*
—*T. c. mexicana*
—*T. c. triunguis*
—*T. c. yucatana*

***Terrapene coahuila*—Coahuilan Box Turtle**

No subspecies recognized

Terrapene nelsoni—Spotted Box
  Turtle
—*T. n. nelsoni*
—*T. n. klauberi*
Terrapene ornata—Ornate Box
  Turtle
—*T. o. ornata*
—*T. o. luteola*
Genus **CUORA**
ASIAN BOX TURTLES
Cuora amboinensis—Southeast
  Asian Box Turtle
—*C. a. amboinensis*
—*C. a. couro*
—*C. a. kamaroma*
Cuora aurocapitata—Yellow-headed
  Box Turtle
No subspecies recognized
Cuora flavomarginata—Yellow-
  margined Box Turtle
—*C. f. flavomarginata*
—*C. f. evelynae*
—*C. f. sinensis*
Cuora galbinifrons—Indochinese
  Box Turtle
No subspecies recognized
Cuora mccordi—McCord's Box
  Turtle
No subspecies recognized
Cuora pani—Pan's Box Turtle
No subspecies recognized
Cuora trifasciata—Chinese Three-
  striped Box Turtle
No subspecies recognized
Cuora yunnanensis—Yunnan Box
  Turtle
No subspecies recognized
Cuora zhoui—Zhou's Box Turtle
No subspecies recognize

The rarest of the box turtles is the Coahuilan Box Turtle, *Terrapene coahuila*, which can only be found at its type-locality, in Coahuila, Mexico.

SUZANNE L. AND JOSEPH T. COLLINS.

ISABELLE FRANCAIS.

Although there are a few commercial breeders of box turtles, specimens are still getting harder and harder to acquire as environmental laws concerning them get tighter and tighter. Photo of a Common Box Turtle, *Terrapene carolina*.

ACQUISITION

In today's herpetological hobby there are many sources at one's disposal through which top-quality box turtle specimens can be acquired. For the keeper who is looking to begin or expand his or her box turtle stock, this is truly good news.

CONSIDERATIONS BEFOREHAND

Before you rush out and find your new box turtle, there are a few things you should think about, if not for your own benefit, then for the benefit of the animal(s) in question.

For example, most box turtles, as you will learn, are best kept outdoors rather than in a cage or a tank. Do you have the space to accommodate this need? If not, then there is a very good chance the animal will respond poorly to captivity and soon perish.

Or, are there any laws in your area that prohibit the keeping of box turtles? As odd as this may sound, it is often true. Take the time to check with your local environmental agency about such things; they will be more than happy to send any and all relevant information to someone who is so willing to abide by the rules. And don't underestimate such authorities—there are many examples of hobbyists being levied with heavy fines and in some cases actual jail time due to their refusal to honor governmental codes concerning herptiles.

Finally, are you aware of the fact that keeping a box turtle in captivity can be a lifelong project? As long as the animal is in good health (which it should be, or else what's the point?) it should live about as long as an ordinary human being. It is a cruel fact of reality, but there are more than a few hobbyists who, after a time, get bored of their pets and begin to neglect them. That's not fair. If (and you have to be honest with yourself) you think you are one of these types of people, at least configure some sort of "backup plan" whereby the animal(s) can be orphaned off to someone else. Otherwise, you will undoubtedly have a friend for life, with all its captive needs and responsibilities resting purely on your shoulders.

PROFESSIONAL BREEDERS

For the most part, this is very probably the best overall source for getting your hands on really top-notch box turtle specimens. The advantages are obvious: you are getting turtles that have been cultivated purely in a domestic environment, which of course does no harm to the natural environment and furthermore sidesteps the considerable hassle of violating collecting laws and so forth. Usually a captive-bred box turtle will do well in the home, feeding and eventually breeding without trouble. It is now almost standard procedure for a professional breeder to not even sell animals that are born sick or have not yet begun to feed regularly (as they have reputations to maintain), so the buyer is virtually guaranteed satisfaction.

You can contact such people through a variety of channels, the most obvious being the popular magazines, societies, journals, or newsletters. There are currently at least three or four box turtle subspecies being bred commercially. If you call or write and ask for a price list, a breeder will be more than happy to accommodate you. The only problem you may run into is where the mail system is concerned. The "normal" postal system in the United States does not permit the shipping of turtles so you

K. H. SWITAK.

Closeup of a scute of a Desert Box Turtle, *Terrapene ornata luteola*. Scutes should always be closely examined on specimens you are thinking of purchasing.

will have to utilize air freight via the airport. This can get costly, sometimes to the point where the charges exceed the monetary value of the turtle(s). It is advised you take all these things into consideration before making a commitment.

PET SHOPS

The second best place to acquire a box turtle is obvious—in a pet store. It will not be hard to track down a pet store that sells herptiles (a collective name for reptiles and amphibians) but it should be made known that in some states the selling of box turtles of any kind through such a place is purely illegal. Before you go out of your mind looking around, call a number of dealers first. You may save yourself a trip.

Another major concern you should have with a pet store is the quality of the animal(s) you are interested in purchasing. It is not at all the author's intention to "slam" pet stores in any way; in fact I have seen many shops over the years that have so impressed me I would gladly endorse them. But the truth of the matter remains that a few others (the much smaller percentage, thank goodness) are, at times, so appalling, condition-wise, that it would hard to believe anyone would want to purchase anything there in the first place.

Cleanliness is the first sign. When you walk inside, don't judge the sanitation by the smell—I know of no pet store that reminds me of a rose-filled meadow. Judge it by more direct means—the tanks themselves for example. In the case of box turtles, you won't be able to study the water mass to any useful degree (as you would with aquatic turtle species) but you can look at the surface of the land area. Are there piles or smearings of feces? Are there bits of food still lying about that are covered in so much mold they could be used to produce penicillin? Do the turtles themselves have dirty shells or swollen eyes? Do they look lethargic and miserable (be careful with this—box turtles aren't known for their spunk. They won't be jumping against the glass when you walk by like a puppy would. This is a matter of "feel")?

Check all skin areas on box turtles before buying them. Photo of a Desert Box Turtle, *Terrapene ornata luteola*.

K. H. SWITAK.

K. H. SWITAK.

A healthy box turtle will be quick and alert, whereas ill specimens will be very limp and lethargic. Photo of a Desert Box Turtle, *Terrapene ornata luteola*.

A good test is to ask the owner, manager, worker, etc., if the animal eats regularly and what exactly its dietary preferences have been. Ask for a demonstration, keeping in mind that sometimes a box turtle will just not be in the food mood and may refuse the meal regardless of its genuine good health. If in your judgment the turtle looks healthy, you may want to take a chance (ask about the return policy). If it eats right in front of you, great. If it doesn't, then you have a decision to make.

WILD COLLECTING

This option really should, and will, be played down to a large degree because we are in an age when respect, awareness, and moral consciousness toward global ecology is very much an issue of great importance. There are many ways to encounter box turtles in the wild without violating any of our natural laws.

For example, in many areas where the wild collection of box turtles is still legal, who says a hobbyist will ever need more than one male and one female? An adult breeding pair will more than suffice any keeping needs you may have and of course gives you the means to propagate them if you wish (which further gives you the means to trade the offspring for other herptiles with your peers later on).

Or, an interesting sideline to the hobby that you may find most gratifying is herpetological photography. As long as I have been doing it myself I can never seem to set up any artificial background scenery that even comes close in simple beauty to that of an animal's natural habitat. They were, after all, meant to be there, so how can you compete with the nature of things? The next time you go out into the woods on a hike or whatever, bring your camera along. If and when you encounter a box turtle, you may want to consider simply photographing it rather than

It is of great importance for you to check around the head of a specimen you are thinking of purchasing. This is often where signs of illness will be most apparent. Photo of a Desert Box Turtle, *Terrapene ornata luteola*.

K. H. SWITAK.

K. T. NEMURAS.

Young box turtles are usually in pretty good shape when offered for sale, but specimens that have been imported, like the Southeast Asian Box Turtle, *Cuora amboinensis*, shown here, should be suspected of ill-health because they may not have taken the traveling very well.

removing it from its home. Besides, many wild-caught box turtles, plainly and simply, do poorly in captivity. I must confess to more than one occasion when I would bring a specimen home only to find it would not eat one damn thing. In those cases you really have no other choice but to return it to its place of origin. Remember—some box turtles live over a hundred years and are very used to their specific surroundings. The last thing they want is to be relocated and will let you know it in a very up-front manner.

SWAP MEETS, ETC.

The final option to be discussed concerns a simple enough idea—going to one of the many herpetological swap meets that seem to be occurring these days. You almost never have to be part of any club or society in order to attend but you should still subscribe to one of the magazines, journals, or newsletters so you will know when such events are scheduled. Even if you live in an area where herpetoculture is a virtually nonexistent hobby, there will still very likely be a place within driving distance where it is.

During these meets, dozens of vendors will set up their wares for show, trade, sale, and sometimes to look for new animals to buy. Most of the animals on display will be captive-bred and will have already proven their reliability as captives (rarely will a vendor bother to bring a "non-choice" specimen to a show because it will not be particularly saleable and simultaneously make him or her look bad). A swap meet is also a good place to bring any "traders" you may have. If you have acquired a breeding pair of box turtles and then propagated them, the excess offspring could be very valuable currency during such a meet. Think of it—you have a newborn male and female Eastern Box Turtle, *Terrapene carolina carolina*, and across the room you spot a table with a pair of newborn Ornate Box Turtles, *Terrapene ornata*. There's a good chance a simple trade can be made and you will have obtained a new pair that will also be ready for breeding in a few years. And the best part is they didn't even cost you a dime.

HOUSING

As I have mentioned previously, the box turtles are a race of chelonians that, for the most part, do not enjoy the confines of captivity and thus must be given as much room as possible. Therefore, it is up to the keeper to provide this to the best of his or her abilities. I am aware that not everyone, myself included, has acres and acres of land that they can just go building turtle pens on. But there are other options.

purpose your heart desires, it would be much to both your and the turtle's benefit to build an outdoor enclosure for them. It will be much better for the animals's well-being in every respect.

The area need not be very large. 15 ft square is more than adequate, even for multiple specimens. What you should do first is mark off the area with small posts in each corner and suspend a line of string between each. Then, dig a trench about a foot

Ideally, most box turtles should be kept outside during the warmer months. Many specimens will only respond well to captive living if given this type of freedom of space. Photo of a Yellow-headed Box Turtle, *Cuora aureocapitata*.

R. D. BARTLETT.

ENCLOSURES

Keeping a Box Turtle Outside

If in fact you do happen to have a nice-sized piece of land and can spare some of it for whatever

deep around the area, just wide enough to sink a plank of wood. This wood will make up the walls in the pen and must be buried fairly deep since box turtles can dig and may try to work their way under and out to freedom. It is advised you simply buy a few 2 x 6 ft or 2 x 8 ft planks (2 x 4 ft is also acceptable but 2 x 6 and 2 x 8 ft are better). These can be attached together, built up gradually to make a wall of proper height. That height, for ordinary adult box turtles, need not be over two feet. They can't scale the walls, after all!

Once you have built the basic enclosure (with some of the wood buried to stop them from "going under the wall,") you should cut small triangles (about a foot long on each side) and nail them on top of the enclosure corners. This is simply a safety precaution taken since many box turtles, although they can't climb a flat, upright surface, can still shimmy between the corners. They are very determined, remember, and will take these opportunities if you offer them.

There are of course many implements that need to be included in any captive animal's tank, the box turtles not withstanding. The water bowl, for example, should be strong and sturdy because box turtles can be very clumsy and will constantly knock over more insipid ones. Most keepers like to use a long, shallow tray instead of a water bowl because the box turtles may also like to bathe in it as well as drink from it.

Natural plants are also a nice touch and will be a source of great pleasure to your pets. It is of course easiest for the keeper to provide plants of a perennial nature as opposed to bothering with new ones every season, and I have found that the leafier the plant, the better. You can either place them right into the soil, or sink a plant with the pot and all.

Finally, a natural-looking hiding area can be made easily enough with a bunch of large rocks (purchased at any landscaper's supply house) cemented together with a little ingenuity and some basic masonry skill. This is an inexpensive way to provide a box turtle with a beautiful shelter that not only blends in perfectly with their surroundings but will be a permanent structure.

Free Run of a Small Room

As odd as it may be for non-box turtle enthusiasts to imagine, there are more than a few keepers who allow their pets the freedom of running about in a room all their own. Although this is a form of keeping a box turtle inside, it is one of the better ways of doing so. It is probably the option most often resorted to in the case of keepers who live in major cities like New York, San Francisco, etc., where natural land is simply in short supply. Most of these people rent apartments and thus their choices are limited to begin with.

If you live in a temperate zone and are keeping a box turtle indoors with no intention of hibernating it, you are going to have to supply some form of heat if you expect the animal to live well. A heating pad is a very popular item in the herpetocultural hobby these days. Heating pads seem to use very little electricity and can be placed virtually anywhere. I would suggest you set up some sort of box as a "home base" for the box turtle(s) and place the heater there. It's almost like those silly little cat and dog beds; a place the turtles can call their own.

In the summer, of course, one does not have to worry about heat so much, but there are still a few details to keep in mind. For example, box turtles seem to love

If you have the time, patience, and skill, you can build a nice house for land turtles like the one shown here.

If you do build a turtle house, be sure to hinge the roof so you can easily get inside for maintenance purposes and so on.

Also be sure you include a number of climate-control devices like those shown here. A thermometer is always a useful monitoring device in the keeping of any captive herptiles.

If you have the space, it is best to keep land turtles in walled-in outdoor enclosures. Simple boundaries can be made from stones (for the base) and fencing (for the walls).

Some keepers will go to great expense and trouble to house their land turtles, and although such setups may seem a bit extravagant to some, the keepers who have this much passion for their pets should be supported and applauded.

If, after a time, you feel you have mastered the keeping of box turtles outside, you may want to consider moving on to tortoises next. Tortoises are very rewarding and enjoyable pets. All photos on this and the preceding page by Patti Ann Rutledge.

Adult box turtles need to be kept outside more so than the young do. They are too large to be kept in a tank and they like to wander. Without the space to do so, they will fare very poorly in captivity. Photo of an Eastern Box Turtle, *Terrapene carolina carolina*. Photo by Mella Panzella.

PHOTO COURTESY OF FOUR PAWS

A localized heat source will be greatly appreciated by box turtles that are kept indoors.

basking in the sunlight so it would be very much appreciated if you left a window open during the warmer seasons; chances are even the most timid specimens will come out and lay under the beam for hours. Along the same lines, a box turtle will sometimes get too hot, and thus you should also give them the same type of shallow pool area mentioned before. They will need it to cool off in.

Of course, the other basic provisions must be kept in mind as well—clean water (at all times), fresh food (offered in a bowl if it is not live, and place the bowl under some newspaper or something similar), and, of course, provide an area where the turtle will learn to defecate regularly (since you would not want turtle messes all over your house, no matter what room the animal was in). You may want to approach the defecation problem from a different starting point—by learning where the turtles go most often and then simply placing the paper there. I have heard of a few keepers who have actually litter box-trained their box turtles but the process takes much time and patience, which some of us may not have.

Finally, it should be pointed out

that the provision of natural sunlight is an essential facet of turtle keeping, so if you cannot provide an indoor box turtle with direct rays (they cannot be blocked, screened, or filtered in any way), then purchasing a full-spectrum bulb from a pet store is a must. These are somewhat expensive but a turtle with most certainly die

Cage liners can be used with neonatal box turtles. The liners are both attractive and easy to clean.

PHOTO COURTESY OF FOUR PAWS

without one. The rays give the turtles their much-needed vitamin D3 which spearheads proper bone growth and shell formation. You should leave the light on for about six to eight hours everyday, since that is the prescribed photoperiod for the genus.

The Turtle Table

A fairly clever idea, there is a wonderfully detailed article on building a turtle table in the July/ August 1990 issue of *Reptile and Amphibian Magazine* by David T. Kirkpatrick. What a turtle table is, in essence, is a table that has been converted into an area for smaller land turtles whose owners do not have land areas to spare and cannot give their pets the run of an entire room.

The main ideology involves taking a table, cutting some rectangular holes in it, then recessing a few shallow pans or tubs, these of

For land-dwelling turtles, bark nuggets make a good substrate. Bark nuggets can be purchased in bulk and are easy to work with.

PHOTO COURTESY OF FOUR PAWS

course being filled with soil and plants, a shallow water area for cooling off, a container for food and another for drinking water, and so on. Of course, the *entire* table is not cut up this way because space has to be left for the turtles to roam around on. There are also clear plastic sheets (the walls) attached to the rims of the table so the turtles can't escape. There are many other tiny details and options you have at your disposal but that's the general idea. Naturally you will not want to use a table that is in pristine condition but you may want to consider scouring yard sales and thrift shops. Either way, the turtle table is certainly a superb idea for people have box turtles and limited space options. Finally, don't forget the provision of the full-spectrum bulb since the turtles will obviously not have sufficient contact with natural sunlight and thus will need this very badly.

Screen covers are probably the most sensible tank tops you can use with small box turtles being kept in glass aquariums.

PHOTO COURTESY OF FOUR PAWS

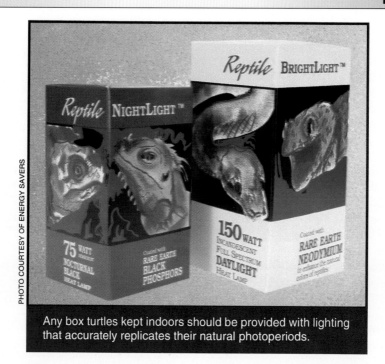

PHOTO COURTESY OF ENERGY SAVERS

Any box turtles kept indoors should be provided with lighting that accurately replicates their natural photoperiods.

Glass Aquariums

The final option, and certainly the last resort, is the old standby, the glass aquarium. I strongly suggest a keeper only take this route when he or she absolutely has to, and even then keep an eye out for a better one.

Of course, it goes without saying that very few adults can be kept in a glass tank, even a large one like a 55-gallon. Smaller box turtles (neonates and yearlings) can be kept in number in something like a 20-gallon but as for the full-grown specimens I would advise only one per tank this size and no more.

The tank can be furnished with all the standard stuff—soil for the bedding, a small water bowl, a hidebox, etc.—and should have a full-spectrum light placed overhead with nothing to block its rays.

CLEANING

Of all the elements to good husbandry that a keeper can develop skills for, perhaps the most important is attention to cleanliness. Let's face it—how well would you

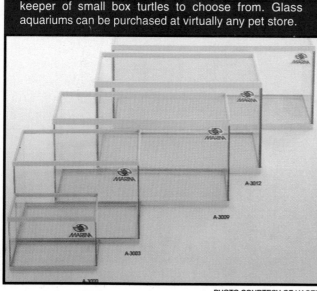

There are a number of glass aquarium sizes for the keeper of small box turtles to choose from. Glass aquariums can be purchased at virtually any pet store.

PHOTO COURTESY OF HAGEN

survive if placed in filthy surroundings? Cleanliness is the most important thing a keeper can do to prevent diseases from occurring and is a responsibility that simply cannot be ignored.

Since there are so many housing choices in the case of box turtles,

of bleach, then rinsed thoroughly in cold. Pans, water bowls, etc., all qualify.
3) Feces should be removed as soon as they are spotted. The area should then also be scrubbed clean or germs will grow with remarkable alacrity.

J. VISSER.

Hatchling and very young box turtles are really the only specimens that can be kept in glass aquariums. Once they are larger, however, it is only fair to let them roam about in free spaces. Photo of a young Southeast Asian Box Turtle, *Cuora amboinensis*.

only the general rules for sanitation can be applied:
1) A good cleaning should be performed at least once a week, perhaps every two weeks in the case of outdoor enclosures. Design a schedule for yourself and stick to it.
2) Anything that can be cleaned and returned should be washed in hot, soapy water with a small amount

4) Don't be afraid to actually wash off the turtles as well. They may need it and some will actually appreciate it. All sorts of gunk can adhere to a box turtle's shell. If you undertake this practice as a normal step during each cleaning you can almost always squelch further problems before they even have a chance to really begin developing.

FEEDING

If I were hard-pressed to give a totally honest evaluation of the box turtles's overall performance in captivity in regards to diet, I would have to say they can be among the most difficult and unpredictable of feeders, although "fussy" might be a better word if I were asked to cut it down to just one.

A lot of this has to do with environment. If you do not provide a box turtle with exactly the surroundings it is hoping for, there is a better than average chance the animal will refuse food completely. Furthermore, a keeper cannot, in the case of box turtles, take the attitude that "when it gets hungry enough, it'll eat," because that is simply untrue. As difficult as it may be for civilized life forms like ourselves to understand, a box turtle would rather cease eating altogether and die rather than be in a situation it doesn't like, even if that situation is a seemingly pleasant one. It is important for a keeper to know that a box turtle will have to be kept in a captive scenario it approves of before it can be expected to accept food regularly. With most other turtles, this does not seem to be so much of an issue (particularly aquatics—they would eat your fingers off if you gave them half the chance), but it is with *Terrapene*, and thus a good keeper should learn as much about the provision of their correct captive habitat as possible before even obtaining one.

Perhaps the nicest aspect of box turtle feeding is the fact that most of them have a highly varied diet; there are many things a keeper can offer them. Photo of an Ornate Box Turtle, *Terrapene ornata*. Photo by Mella Panzella.

FOOD ITEMS

The list of items that have been recorded as accepted box turtle food items seems endless, which is of course good news for a keeper that has finally persuaded its pet to eat. Keep in mind, however, that the main reason a large list is being given here is because many times a box turtle will show a great liking for a certain

used the "spark" a captive turtle's feeding response into action. I have kept many a turtle that would not eat anything else but these slimy little things, and then, after a time, the same turtle would begin taking other items as well. I like to refer to earthworms as the "base" food for carnivorous turtles. You may find this to be true in time as well.

MICHAEL GILROY

Even box turtles that seem to be fussy feeders at first will usually accept earthworms. Many imported box turtles, like the Yellow-margined Box Turtle, *Cuora flavomarginata*, shown here, will have to be "sparked" into feeding in thiš manner.

Earthworms can be obtained a number of ways. The simplest, of course, is to just go out and dig up your own (provided you live in an area where they occur naturally). In the warmer months, worms can be found by turning over

item but totally refuse others, and then another specimen will show preferences that are completely opposite. The point is, there are many choices, so if your box turtle does not like one food, the problem often lies in the simple fact that you haven't found what it "wants" yet. I know it sounds irritating and troublesome for you but it is simply an aspect of box turtles that the keepers of such have to deal with.

Earthworms

Of all the food items turtles of any kind are offered in captivity, the one they all seem to take almost without hesitation is the earthworm.

Often, earthworms are the food

moist logs or by digging with your fingers into moist soil. Moisture is obviously the key here. You won't have to dig deep; only a few inches at most. I myself have found hundreds of them in mulch, woodchip, and wet leaf piles.

If you are fortunate enough to have unlimited access to a pile of organic trash like this, a good method for using it to its maximum potential is to place a piece of wet material on the top of the mound (burlap or an old bedsheet, for example). Wait about two or three days, then turn it over and harvest your stock. This is a very common technique for earthworm acquisition and can be used extensively. When one spot seems to be producing less and less it is obviously becoming overtly depleted, in which case you should simply remove the material and place it elsewhere. If you keep up with this ideology dogmatically, in time you should have a continuous flow.

It should be pointed out that if you don't have to, don't bother trying to maintain or even propagate your own earthworm stock in captivity as this can be very difficult, stressful, and ultimately frustrating. If you have regular access to a worm culture in the wild, use it. However, if you have live in an area where earthworms are not in abundance, or in fact do not occur at all, you can always try locating a fisherman's bait shop. There, they should have worms of all types and sizes. If that proves fruitless as well, try contacting one of the many livefood suppliers who advertise in the herp magazines, newsletters, and so forth. Often, the worms you buy will be frozen rather than live. Be sure they are individually wrapped or else they will freeze together in one revolting mass, making it impossible to thaw just one

MICHAEL GILROY

Once acclimated to captive living, a box turtle can be fed right from the keeper's hand. Photo of a Yellow-margined Box Turtle, *Cuora flavomarginata*.

no choice but to keep them alive in captivity for whatever reason, give them a large box of soft soil and cover the surface with freshly decaying leaf litter every four or five days. Placing them in a refrigerator is also a plus as this slows them down and makes their needs less demanding (although who knows what Aunt Bessie will say when she opens the door to grab a beer and sees a boxful of large, slimy worms squirming about).

If on the other hand you happen to or two. And speaking of thawing, the proper method involves soaking the worm(s) in a bowl of warm (not too warm) water for a few minutes.

Insects

Simply calling this category "insects" is certainly being very general about it, I realize, but then again, that's as close to the truth as I can get. The fact is, there aren't many insects a wild box turtle will come across and not eat.

Crickets, for example, will be scooped up and gulped down with great eagerness. So will all sorts of flies, grasshoppers, spiders, and so on. The first of these items, the crickets, are easy enough to get a hold of; its almost impossible to imagine a pet shop that carries herps and doesn't sell crickets. (If you actually do have trouble finding these, try ordering them from any of the cricket farms—yes, cricket farms—that advertise in herp mags and so forth.) But the other items, however—the grasshoppers, locusts, etc.—may be things you will have to find on your own.

The nice thing about most insects is that they can be sprinkled with multi-vitamin powder before being served to box turtles. This is a great way to supplement the turtle's diet and will be covered further on in this chapter.

As I said before, insects of all kinds appeal to box turtles, and that reminds of an incident I remember that occurred on a warm summer night in 1991:

A friend of mine, Keith, was coming home from work one night when he spotted a large male Eastern Box Turtle, *Terrapene carolina carolina*, crossing the road. Being of a kindly nature and not wishing to see it smushed, he stopped his truck and ran out to get it. He placed it in the truck bed and continued on.

He phoned me about an hour later from a friend's garage and asked if I wanted the animal. Generally I prefer not to work with wild-caught

specimens unless they are the specific focus of my studies, so I told him no but I would still like the opportunity to photograph it. The agreement was then made that I would come down and take the shots immediately so he could return it later that night to the woods that transversed the road where it was found.

When I arrived, I was somewhat bewildered to find Keith holding the animal up with its head almost touching a section of the doorway

Crickets are an excellent food item for box turtles, and their nutritional value can be further enhanced if you sprinkle some vitamin powder on them.

frame he was standing in. Inquiring as to what was happening, he shushed me and told me to just watch.

And it was then, much to my amazement, that I saw this freshly wild-caught turtle lunge its head forward and grab a large beetle right off the framing! Keith told me it had been grabbing all the "bugs" it saw since he brought it in. It seems it all began when Keith saw a small cricket climbing across the hood of his truck and was curious as to what the turtle would do if he got near it. Using the same lateral holding technique, he leaned the animal down and sure enough the animal grabbed it. Just goes to show you, if given the right items, even freshly caught specimens will eat with enthusiasm.

Fruits and Vegetables

Probably the easiest items for any box turtle keeper to acquire are fruits and vegetables. It should most definitely be pointed out, however, that many box turtles will not accept either of these during the first three to six (and sometimes even more) years of their life.

PAUL FREED

Grasshoppers may be a little more difficult than crickets for the average keeper to acquire, but they too are a highly nutritional meal for captive box turtles.

The most obvious place to obtain fruits and vegetables is at your local supermarket or roadside produce stand. The turtles will rarely be picky about the quality of the foods but you should of course endeavor to provide reasonably high-quality materials nevertheless. The nice thing about fruits and vegetables is that they are relatively inexpensive and can be stored in your refrigerator for weeks at a time. Some keepers even go so far as to actually freeze cucumbers, beets, apples, etc., but in my opinion they are so easy to get a hold of fresh, there is really no reason to resort to freezing.

A warning of sorts that should be noted here is that you will probably end up with a box turtle as individual in its fruit and vegetable tastes as any human being could be. For example, I know of a woman who kept a box turtle that would only take cantaloupe, fruit-wise. Then she obtained another specimen (that had been injured and was lying on the side of the road with one bloody foot), that (after recovery) would gladly eat apples but refused cantaloupe completely. One fruit group that seems very popular with box turtles of all species is the berries. Bananas have also garnered repeatedly positive results.

As for vegetables, I can only advise that the keeper try everything he or she can get their hands on. Carrots are quite popular, as are radishes and beets. Corn does not seem to go over too well, but again, maybe you already own a box turtle that gobbles corn right off the cob.

One interesting approach that I have utilized myself involves the creation of a "box turtle food mix" whereby the keeper simply takes a number of fruits and vegetables that their particular turtle has shown a liking for and then blends or chops them up into one conglomerated mass. This mass can then be kept in a small container in the refrigerator and spooned out until needed. You can even sprinkle some multi-vitamin powder into the mix and the turtles probably won't even notice. You may have to submit to some experimentation before you find your own best "recipe" but once you do you will find the convenience irresistible.

Hard-boiled Eggs

I must confess I was shocked when I first saw a box turtle take a hard-boiled egg. Not because it was such an amazing visual showing but

MICHAEL GILROY

Mealworm beetles can be cultured in a keeper's home and "gut-loaded" for added nutritional value. Gut-loading simply involves raising the beetles on a high vitamin diet.

because I couldn't help but wonder how they ever developed such an appeal for them. I have never come across a box turtle in a chicken coop, bird's nest, etc., although I eventually learned that they do occasionally forage in these places for food, but whether or not they come across chickens that lay eggs already hard-boiled is another matter entirely (the chances seem slim).

Of course, for a keeper, a hard-boiled egg is not something all too difficult to provide. The problem is, it really isn't a complete nutritional meal and should only be given in supplement (like the fruit and vegetable mixture mentioned before, for example).

A final note the reader may find interesting is that there is no need to remove a hard-boiled egg's shell before giving it to your box turtle because they will eat that too. I was also quite stunned when I first learned this, but sure enough, when I tried it on my own stock, I witnessed a large male munch down that hard white coating with no problems whatsoever.

Carrion

The sight of a box turtle crushed in the road is truly a saddening sight, but all emotions aside, there is something interesting to be noted about the corpses—often they are lying very near to something else squished in the road. This always made me wonder about the degree of coincidence involved, then I realized there probably wasn't any. These turtles were trying to make a meal from the remains of some other creature whose luck ran out.

Obviously a keeper is not going to go out with a paint scraper and remove every dead thing he or she spots on the way home from work but there are still a few items you can provide within dignified limits.

Dead mice, for example. If you are a varied herpetoculturist and keep snakes as well, chances are you have one that eats mice. Often times you will end up with a mouse that, for whatever reason, was not accepted by your snake(s). Don't throw it out; give it to your box turtle. This applies to rats as well.

Or perhaps you have a fishtank and one of your stock has passed away. Box turtles often take raw fish. Furthermore, you can always go to a local fish or supermarket and get leftover fish parts at giveaway prices. Ordinary consumers may not have much use for a fish head but a box turtle might.

The nice thing about such items is that they are usually complete in their nutritional value. Bones, heart, liver, etc., everything can be useful to box turtles (as long as the animal was not severely sick, of course). In fact, I knew of a very efficient zookeeper who used to request dead specimens from his peers in other departments for use as box turtle food. He wouldn't even check to see if they were taking them; he'd just toss them into the pen. He knew what they liked, and he was right. The entire concept is grisly, of course, but the main concern is the health of the turtle, and often carrion is a great solution.

KEN LUCAS

A few box turtles may take pillbugs. The appeal of pillbugs is the fact that many people can obtain them right in their own backyard.

Raw Meat

This is perhaps an expensive way to feed a box turtle, but it is nevertheless an option that should be considered a treat or a last resort. Box turtles, particularly very young ones, seem to respond well to bits of roast beef, ham, chicken, and so on. Of course, it is important to make sure whatever meat you give them is not overtly fatty or you will be abusing their cardiovascular system.

Most raw meats can be obtained through supermarkets and are fairly nutritional. They really should be offered with other things, however, and even in those cases only given sparingly at best. Since there are better items a keeper can provide, raw meat should not be on the top of the daily food list unless no other accepted items can be found.

Commercial Foods

Nowadays, with the hobby of herpetoculture growing faster than a muscle on steroids, a couple of companies have come up with products designed just for the feeding needs of a few of the more popular herptiles, and box turtles are among them. Part of the marketing scheme is actually kind of cute—the packages come in low cans (as with moist cat food) or plastic deli cups; almost a "gourmet diet" concept.

But are these items nutritious?

Overall, I'd say yes. Think about it—why would a such a product even been offered if it had no redeeming value whatsoever? There are flaws, however, like expense, for example. Most of these items are not cheap. Furthermore, you really can't offer any on a singular basis; eventually you will have to expand the animal's diet. In summary, I would say most commercial box turtle foods are acceptable and certainly will do them no harm, but the two points mentioned above should be kept clearly in mind.

Vitamin Supplements

For any captive herptile, occasional vitamin supplementation is crucial. The reasons are obvious—to give the animal a complete nutritional profile.

Most vitamin supplements can be purchased in either tablet or capsule form. Both of these are good because you can either grind the tablets into powder or separate the capsule and get the powder that way. This then can be sprinkled on food items. All owners of land turtles should be thankful it's that easy—there is a considerable amount of trouble involved in getting such powders to adhere to the food of aquatic turtles.

It is advised you give your box turtle a light sprinkling of multi-vitamins about once every month, perhaps every couple of weeks if the foods you are providing are truly low in certain elements. Be careful not to

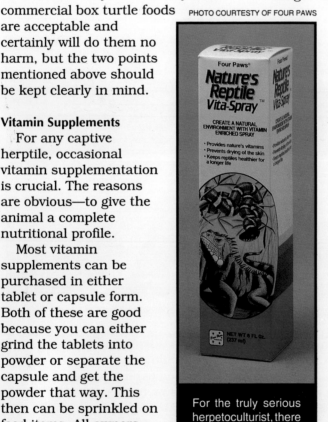

PHOTO COURTESY OF FOUR PAWS

For the truly serious herpetoculturist, there are vitamin sprays available. They can be used with many reptile and amphibian species.

overdo it, though—hypovitaminosis is a disease that has claimed the lives of many captive herptiles.

FEEDING PROBLEMS

Your box turtle won't eat. What can be done? There are a number of things.
1) If the animal you have is wild-caught and you are keeping it indoors, perhaps its time to keep it outdoors (unless of course you live in a temperate zone and this is happening during the wintertime). Often I find this to be the main gripe of captive box turtles—they want to live in a situation that suggests captivity as little as possible. Build a pen for them in your backyard, if you have one. The way that being outside affects some box turtles is truly amazing.

Example: a friend of mine had three Eastern Box Turtles, *Terrapene carolina carolina*, that were all captured in the wild. He kept them for about two weeks and none ate even once. Naturally, he began to grow worried for their health and considered returning them, which of course is standard procedure.

Then, another friend in Pennsylvania said he had good luck with wild-caught "boxer" and asked if he could give them a try for a week. Unlike my friend, he planned on keeping them in an outdoor enclosure that he had built and kept box turtles in before.

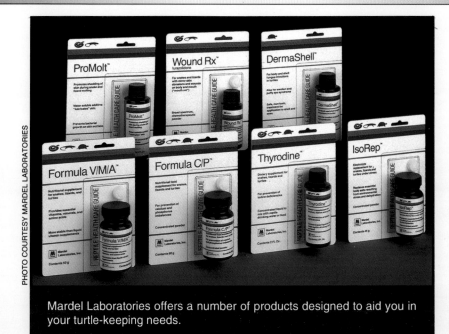

PHOTO COURTESY MARDEL LABORATORIES

Mardel Laboratories offers a number of products designed to aid you in your turtle-keeping needs.

Sure enough, within a day or two, he started tossing food items in and they took them (and with great eagerness I might add). To this day, all three still live in their little outdoor pen in Pennsylvania and still eat like starved wolves.

The obvious point of this story is that something as simple as housing considerations can play a major role in a box turtle's eating habits. If you end up with a specimen that seems unwilling to eat and you know you cannot supply it with the proper facilities, release it. There's no productive value in taking any other approach.

2) Perhaps you're not giving the animal the right items. Earlier in this chapter was a long list of things box turtles have been known to eat, with a discussion concerning each one. If you haven't read through it yet, then do so. You may find a suggested item that turns out to be the solution. And don't be afraid to go beyond what I've listed in this book. If you think your turtle will accept something and you are

sure it will not be detrimental to its health then go right ahead and offer it.

3) Consider the time of year. Remember that some turtles hibernate; just because you're keeping their temperatures up doesn't mean they'll act normally. Some box turtles have biological clocks so sensitive they will honor them regardless of outside influences.

4) Be sure the area they are kept in is clean. Even an animal that takes food right from your fingers may not eat in filthy surroundings. Can you blame them?

5) Finally, you may have to consider the possibility that you have a sick box turtle. In such a case, the only correct thing to do is bring it to a vet, otherwise it may die. There is a sickness and disease chapter in this booklet but it is designed to help you understand and occasionally diagnose a health problem; it is not there to encourage you to perform treatments

A number of *Cuora* species are presently being bred in captivity, and although such specimens can be expensive, they are nevertheless far superior than those that have been wild-caught. Photo of Pan's Box Turtle, *Cuora pani*, by Mella Panzella.

Although there are not a lot of breeders or keepers who breed box turtles on a regular basis, the fact is they are not terribly difficult to breed either way. The key, really, is patience, and, of course, a thorough understanding of the captive techniques.

PREPARATIONS

Since breeding in captivity is simply a parallel to breeding in the wild, we must follow the chronology of the natural process and take things one step at a time. The first major stage in box turtle breeding, at least concerning those species which live in the more temperate regions, is correct hibernation. But before that is attempted, there are a few details that must first be attended to.

For one, you really have to make a keen judgment call as to whether or not the turtles you have are in any condition to hibernate. The keeper must remember that hibernation in any form is a strain on an animal's health. During hibernation, a turtle will literally shut its body functions down to their bare minimum and live off all energies stored during the active season. If you have a specimen that has not eaten well and looks malnourished, then hibernating it may be a fatal decision.

Furthermore, once you have chosen your "hibernatable" stock, you cannot simply drop their ambient temperature and expect that to be the end of it. It is crucial when hibernating any herptile, whether it be a snake, lizard, turtle, or whatever, that its system is completely devoid of all wastes or else those wastes will burn through the walls of the internal organs that have been "turned off" by the reduced temperature.

A simple, easy, and reliable way of assuring that a turtle is completely

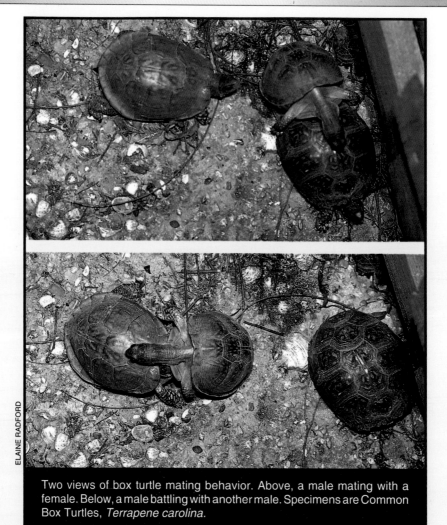

ELAINE RADFORD

Two views of box turtle mating behavior. Above, a male mating with a female. Below, a male battling with another male. Specimens are Common Box Turtles, *Terrapene carolina*.

"empty" is by first stopping its feedings about two weeks prior to the start of the hibernating period, then bathing it daily in warm water for about four hours at a time. These baths are the key to getting their systems "clean."

Finally, it is ill-advised to try hibernating species that do not hibernate naturally. Some of the Central and South American subspecies, for example, will simply go through a period of estivation whereby their bodies will endure a short "rest." This seems to be adequate for them and should be replicated faithfully in captivity.

ARTIFICIAL HIBERNATION

Many hobbyists wonder why a reptile needs to be hibernated at all. If they are in fact kept in a warm, clean environment, wouldn't they simply function normally anyway?

Well, yes and no. Yes, if you keep a box turtle warm, feed it, keep it clean, etc., of course it will do fine, but if you wish to breed it, you cannot overlook the necessity of a winter rest period. This time is essential to a box turtle's reproductive cycle because it helps spark off the hormones that make fertility possible. There are of course the occasional stories about keepers who have never hibernated their stock and still got them to breed with success, but these instances are very rare at best and certainly not dependable references.

The ideal hibernating temperature for cold-region box turtles is about 45°F (7°C). This can vary slightly in either an upper or lower direction, of course, but if dips too low, deaths could occur; too high, and the animals may not hibernate at all. The ideal time period involved is about three or four months. In some wild places they will hibernate longer, but the time reduction will not harm them.

Since box turtles are land-dwelling creatures, it is best that they be hibernated outdoors. Of course, this is not always possible in the case of every hobbyist, so I will try to offer suggestions concerning both indoor and outdoor accommodations.

Outdoor Hibernation

If in fact you do have a large area of land at your disposal, the proper facilities can be created by simply digging a hole in the ground about four foot square (per pair—increase width about one foot for each additional specimen), then layering the walls with some study mesh screening. On the floor, lay about a three to six-inch layer of vermiculite (which will help retain moisture) and cover this with another sheet of sturdy screening. Then add in a thin bedding of straw or hay (no more than one or two inches) and place the turtles inside. Cover them up with more straw, hay, peat or sphagnum moss, and even some dried leaves. Finally, cover the "top" (which is level with the ground surface) with another sheet of screening, and add on a pile of more leaves and hay (about six to

Standard mating position for the North American box turtles. Shown is a pair of Common Box Turtles, *Terrapene carolina*.

B. KAHL

ten inches of it).

Once you have set the turtles up in their hibernaculum, do not disturb them, as this can be very dangerous to their health. Also, you may want to consider enclosing the immediate area around the den, if you have not done so already, for the purpose of keeping out small animals, etc.

Indoor Hibernation

If you are keeping your box turtles indoors and have no choice but to hibernate them there as well, don't worry. As long as there is an area of your dwelling that gets reliably cold during the winter months, you will be able to accomplish what needs to be done.

The best containers to use, short of building your own, are wooden crates, like the kind used to ship fruits and vegetables in. One advantage to them is the fact that they are already aerated, which is important. However, if you cannot locate one, simply build a large wooden cube (about three foot square), and make sure you drill some airholes in the sides.

Fill the box with the same peat/moss/sphagnum mixture and basically replicate what you would be doing outside. One of the advantages to hibernating box turtles indoors is that you can occasionally check on them with greater ease than if they were buried in the ground. Of course, you don't want to do this too often or you may disturb them to the point where their cycle will be badly thrown off. Only during the monthly check or in cases of extreme emergency should a hibernating turtle be disturbed.

Hatchling example of the beautiful Three-toed Box Turtle, *Terrapene carolina triunguis.*

R. D. BARTLETT

K. T. NEMURAS

Newborn box turtles are more carnivorous than adults, and you will probably have to crush up their food for them. Photo of a hatchling Eastern Box Turtle, *Terrapene carolina carolina*.

CONSIDERATIONS AFTER HIBERNATION

When the hibernation period draws to a close and it is time to "wake" your box turtles, remember that their ambient temperature needs to be raised much in the same fashion that it was lowered—slowly. Do not simply remove them from their "dens" and place them in warm areas. This will shock them.

Also, do not be surprised or alarmed if recently "awoken" box turtles have no interest in food. They will be disoriented for a day or two afterward and will need time to readjust. Many will look scrawny and malnourished. This is natural, considering the circumstances. Be patient and feed them when they are ready. Keep the males and females separate during this critical period before actual breeding begins, as this will be advantageous (males often

lose interest in females they are too familiar with). About a week or two after they have returned to their normal habits, breeding can begin.

THE CAPTIVE BREEDING PROCESS

The actual copulatory habits of the box turtles has been fairly well-documented. It begins when a male, almost completely in her shell, allowing just a small slit for viewing. The male then begins moving around her, darting his head in and out, and occasionally biting at her. He will perform this bizarre "ritual" for anywhere from 15 minutes to a couple of hours.

When he is ready, he will climb

W. P. MARA

The use of both vermiculite and sphagnum moss seems to work wonderfully in the incubation of turtle eggs.

having developed an interest for a particular female, approaches her, stops directly in front of her (so they are face to face), then raises himself up on all four legs so his plastron is completely suspended. This seems to tell the female that he is planning to mate. She will in turn close herself

For many box turtles, captive-breeding is the only route to continued survival. Many species and subspecies are suffering rapid population declines. Photo of a captive-bred Gulf Coast Box Turtle, *Terrapene carolina major*. Photo by Mella Panzella.

onto her carapace from the back and lean forward until his claws are well out ahead of him. It is at this time that he will bite at the female's head, indicating that he wants her to open up the lower rear portion of her shell. If she is receptive, he will then slip his two hind claws between her shell and carapace, after which time the female will close back up slightly, trapping the male's claws inside. He can then press his tail against hers until their vents meet and push off her shell, putting himself in a vertical position.

For the sake of assurance, it would be a good idea for a keeper to separate pairs after each mating, then re-introduce them every three or four days in the hopes that they might mate again. This is a common practice that encourages the possibility of fertilization.

EGGLAYING, EGG CARE, AND CARE OF YOUNG

When a mother box turtle is ready to lay her eggs, you will have to give her plenty of room in which to do it, and that includes depth. If the turtle is not kept outdoors (in which case she will fare for herself), give her a very large box (floor space-wise; height is virtually meaningless) filled with soft soil. She will dig her own nest, lay the eggs, and so on.

If you want to incubate the eggs yourself, remove them carefully (they must always sit in the exact position in which they were laid) and place them in a container filled with moistened vermiculite. The eggs can be buried about three-quarters their size, and then covered with a further layer of slightly moist sphagnum moss. Remember to keep the substrate moist but not wet. Carefully check it every few days.

Incubation time can vary, but somewhere around eight weeks is fairly normal for most box turtles, give or take a few. The young will be very small and need their food crushed up for them. Almost all species will be fairly carnivorous during this time; something to keep in mind when selecting food for them. They will also, of course, need plenty of full-spectrum lighting for bone growth, shell development, and so on.

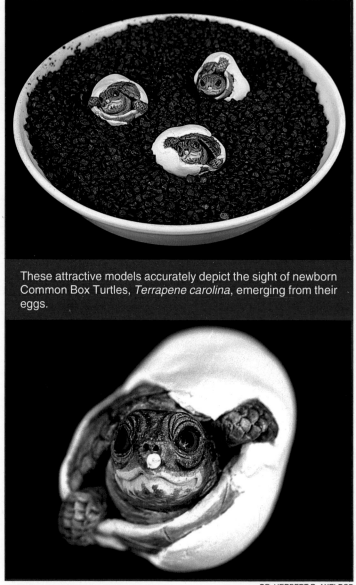

These attractive models accurately depict the sight of newborn Common Box Turtles, *Terrapene carolina*, emerging from their eggs.

DR. HERBERT R. AXELROD

SICKNESS AND HEALTH

It is of course the number one concern of every box turtle enthusiast to keep his or her stock in peak health. The problem is, many captive reptiles are highly susceptible to disease. The fact that most of them have been snatched from their natural surroundings and placed in a world totally alien to them does not help matters any. As close to sterile as we would like to think our own habitations are, there are still innumerable disease-organisms that captive box turtles can pick up which, while being basically harmless to us, can do them a great deal of harm.

Naturally a keeper cannot shield his or her turtles from everything, but to not try is a crime. It is your duty as a hobbyist to provide them with quarters that are as clean as clean can be. This is one of the many aspects of something called preventive medicine. In essence, preventive medicine is just what you would imagine the two words to mean: measures taken to prevent the occurrence of a problem, so rather than combat an illness when it strikes, you do what you have to in order to avoid it in the first place.

TECHNIQUES IN PREVENTIVE MEDICINE

An ordinary herpetoculturist is obviously not going to be able to perform the majority of tasks a veterinarian can, but he or she can most certainly master preventive medicine techniques. Perhaps that is the saddest part of it—preventive measures are really so simple and yet the self-discipline needed to perform them is what many hobbyists lack.

For example, keeping a box turtle's quarters clean. No matter where you end up housing your box turtle (inside or outside), you still have to attend to cleaning duties on a regular basis. Many keepers imagine this

only applies to the former case— inside. Not true. A box turtle kept in an outdoor pen needs to have its area sanitized just as much as one that is inside. Granted, it is probably not as difficult or time-consuming, but it still must be done.

Cleaning Outdoor Enclosures

If you have a box turtle or a group of box turtles that are being kept in an outdoor enclosure and that enclosure is simply a walled off area of your land, an easy method of "freshening" soil that has been defecated on is to simply remove the inmates and all their belongings (hideboxes, waterbowls, etc.), then just take a shovel and "turn" the soil over. If you are not familiar with this term, the concept is elementary— plunge the shovel into the earth, pull out the small section of dirt, then simply flip it over and, if you wish, pack it back down into the hole and smooth it out. (It might be worth noting here that box turtles seem to enjoy a "looser" substrate over a tightly packed one, so you might want to consider not doing this.)

After you have turned the soil, take all the implements you removed and wash them thoroughly in warm, soapy water, rinsing in cold. Finally, you might want to consider bathing the box turtles themselves. Many will not mind this at all, and frequent washing of a box turtle's shell will help keep fungal growth to a minimum.

Cleaning Box Turtle Tanks

If your specimens are kept in a tank, remove the occupants and all implements, wash the tank in warm soapy water and rinse in cold, then wash the implements and, again, if you wish, wash the turtles themselves. If you have a substrate like soil, it should be replaced. If it is something like gravel, wash it as you would any other replaceable item.

It is a good idea for you to faithfully keep a log of every function you perform concerning your pets. This log can be in the form of a diary, a notebook, a small hand-held tape recorder, or, the choice that I have utilized for years, a large desk calendar. The latter truly is a wonderfully easy and convenient way to keep records, but it should be mentioned that the only type to use are those which give you a small box for each day with space in which to write your data. I have developed a sort of "shorthand" which allows me to economize on the wording of my entries. Most keepers don't have the time to write out long, detailed entries every time one of their pets sneezes or quotes Shakespeare, so a condensed method is quite useful. You can put these calendars in the obvious spot—a desk—or you can tack it to a wall. At the end of each month, tear the respective sheet off, fold it up neatly, label it, and file it away. Whatever you do, don't dispose of it! This kind of information can be priceless in the future.

Most box turtles don't seem to care for handling very much, but if you do handle your specimens, be sure to thoroughly wash your hands afterward. Photo of an Eastern Box Turtle, *Terrapene carolina carolina*.

L. QUINN

JIM MERLI

Box turtles kept outdoors should not only have their enclosures cleaned, but their shells should be gently washed as well. All sorts of filth can build up on the shell of a turtle that is kept outside. Photo of a group of Common Box Turtles, *Terrapene carolina*.

COMMON DISEASES OF CAPTIVE BOX TURTLES

Accidents

If a box turtle is roaming around the woods somewhere, looking for some nice fat earthworms, what do you think the odds are that it might burn itself on a heat lamp or be attacked by an aggressive house cat? Of course the latter is always possible, but not likely.

In the home, however, these things do happen. More than once a keeper has hefted a box turtle in his or her hand—totally innocently—and then slipped and dropped it on the floor. Many accidents can occur in a domestic setting, and you should be prepared to deal with them when they do.

If one of your box turtles cuts open any of its soft skin areas, swab the area with some hydrogen peroxide and quarantine the animal to a clean glass aquarium with a soft and slightly dampened paper towel bedding. Allowing the animal to remain in an outdoor enclosure will simply produce a dirty wound that will eagerly await infection. In the case of larger wounds, use the peroxide as outlined above, then bandage the wound with some kind of sterile dressing and get the animal to a vet as quickly as possible. In many cases a severe opening may need stitching, and let's face it— unless you are a vet yourself, this is not something you will be able to do.

Sometimes a box turtle will get a split in its shell and maybe even part of the shell will break off completely. The fact that a turtle's carapace is living tissue is one that many enthusiasts are not aware of. When a turtle cracks or loses part of it, he or she will suffer great pain. Fortunately, some remarkable techniques have developed for treating this problem and the recovery rate is most encouraging. If this happens to your box turtle, take it to a vet immediately. It is not something you can treat at home.

Internal Parasites

One of the more common ailments affecting captive turtles is the invasion of internal parasites. A region that gets attacked often is the intestine. The sources of such a problem are many, but lack of cleanliness and the inclusion of "bad foods" are definitely two of the main ones.

If a box turtle has been badly infected, you will see signs in the feces—they will be watery and runny,

Most parasites like to hide where they can't be seen, so always be sure to check over a box turtle's plastron as well as its carapace. Give particular attention to the skin areas. Photo of a Yellow-margined Box Turtle, *Cuora amboinensis*.

K. T. NEMURAS

R. T. ZAPPALORTI

Ticks are among the most common ectoparasites. Fortunately, they are fairly easy to detect and remove.

and sometimes you will even be able to see tiny the tiny creatures themselves. The turtle will usually act much as you might expect, i.e., lethargic and refusing foods, but beware—many turtles have a remarkable constitution and resistance to disease. They may not even show signs of this problem until it has developed to a severe stage.

The most a keeper can do if he or she suspects such a problem is place the turtle in as clean of a surrounding as possible, start it on a diet of reliably good foods (meaning those that are clean and fresh, etc.), and make an appointment with a vet.

External Parasites

Every now and then a keeper will acquire a turtle with a tick or an infestation of mites. While this is an alarming problem in appearance, it is usually one that can be cured with relative ease as long as it hasn't gotten too far out of hand.

Ticks are tiny little creatures that attach themselves most often to a box turtle's soft skin parts and will live off its blood. Upon first seeing one, most keepers may feel compelled to simply grab the tick with a pair of tweezers and just yank it off. Unfortunately, this is not the correct procedure at all. In fact, you may compound the problem with this method. Often a keeper will pull a tick from an animal's skin only to have the tick's head break off and remain, thus causing further infection. The keeper goes on thinking the animal is cured while infection grows worse and worse.

The first step to removing a tick correctly is to dab it with some alcohol or cover it with some petroleum jelly. This will cause it to loosen its grip. Then, grab it with tweezers as close to its head as possible and *gently* pry it off. Swab the remaining wound with hydrogen peroxide for the next three days. You should have no further problems thereafter.

Mites are a bit more difficult to deal with because they are a little harder to detect. They usually occur in large colonies but are so small they can be easily missed. One easy, albeit somewhat morbid, way to detect

Many Asian box turtles are imported with an internal parasite infestation well under way. If you acquire any of these, it is best that you bring it to a vet for immediate examination. Specimen shown is a Chinese Three-striped Box Turtle, *Cuora trifasciata*.

K. T. NEMURAS.

WILLIAM B. ALLEN, JR

An overgrown mandible is a problem often suffered by captive box turtles. The usual cause is a lack of hard foods. If your box turtle has this problem, it will have to be brought to a vet for immediate treatment.

them is by simply holding the turtle up for a moment or two and then seeing if there are any mites left on your hands after you put it back down again. Another method, and a slightly more rational one at that, involves giving the turtles a "surprise inspection" during the night, when the mites are most active.

Once the problem has been realized, the best method of cure is a daily four-hour bath (with the turtle being totally immersed, except for its head of course) for about a week. You can also include a piece of pest strip in an aerated container (so the turtles don't eat the strip) into the turtle's quarters. Also, be sure to clean the quarters thoroughly, repeating the above outlined treatment a week or so later to kill of any newly hatched mites.

Soft Shell

This is undoubtedly one of the deadliest diseases of captive turtles. The main sign are easy enough to spot—a shell that feels like clay. A turtle's shell, as we know, should be hard and sturdy. If it isn't, then there is a problem. Soft shell is almost always caused by a severe lack of calcium in a turtle's diet. One way calcium is obtained by a box turtle in nature is by exposure to sunlight, which is usually represented in captivity by either a full-spectrum light bulb or, in the case of box turtles being kept in outdoor pens, by the genuine article, the sun itself.

The most common reason turtles suffer from this horrible ailment is because of a shameful degree of neglect by the keeper. Sometimes a hobbyist will purchase a box turtle and its shell is already soft. In this case it probably is the pet store, breeder, or distributor who is at fault. They may have kept the animal in a dark and tiny cage expecting to sell it "any day now."

The best way to cure a box turtle of soft shell is by giving it a crash "calcium treatment." This can be executed by the inclusion of calcium supplements in every sector of their lives—in their water, in their lighting, and, of course, in their food. There are quite a number of commercial products designed to do just this. There are even calcium-enriched gels you can rub directly onto their carapaces.

One of the main advantages to keeping box turtles outside is that they will always be exposed to natural sunlight. Photo of an Eastern Box Turtle, *Terrapene carolina carolina*. Photo by K. H. Switak.

A lack of natural sunlight (or full-spectrum light) is probably the most common cause of softening of the shell in box turtles. Photo of a Desert Box Turtle, *Terrapene ornata luteola*. Photo by K. H. Switak.

Since box turtles are generally opportunistic feeders, getting them to take their food with a little calcium powder added on probably won't be so difficult. In the case of adding it into their drinking water, be careful you don't overdo it because some vitamin powders have a pretty strong smell and may alter the water's scent to the point where the turtles will be turned off by it. Finally, if you have a box turtle that is being kept inside, the provision of a full-spectrum light bulb is an absolute necessity.

A final note to the soft shell problem—this disease is very fast-working (especially on younger turtles, who need more calcium in their diet than adults to begin with) and will reach a stage whereby the chances of recovery will be almost nil. If you suspect one of your specimens to have this problem, deal with it at once.

R. D. BARTLETT.

Two examples of hatchling box turtles. Above, a Florida Box Turtle, *Terrapene carolina bauri*. Below, an Ornate Box Turtle, *Terrapene ornata ornata*.

R. D. BARTLETT.

THE GENUS *CUORA*

Although most hobbyists in the United States are only familiar with one genera of box turtles—*Terrapene*—the fact of the matter is there is a second genus that not only has more species, but is slowly becoming more and more popular—*Cuora*, also known as the Asian box turtles. It has been my plan from the outset to write a brief but detailed and completely separate chapter concerning the care and history of these interesting little creatures. I did not wish to simply "throw them into the mix" as I wrote about *Terrapene* since the two are not all that alike regardless of the

well imagine, quite large. It covers most of southeastern China, stretches west to Yunnan, and then skips across to the Ryukyu and Hainan Islands.

Asian box turtles can be most easily recognized by either very high or very low carapaces; there are no real intermediates. They enjoy semi-aquatic habitats (swamps, shallow ponds and streams, temporary pools, irrigated fields, etc.) and spend most of their active time during the daylight hours.

CAPTIVE HOUSING
Since most of species of *Cuora* are generally not very large (at least

Although the Asian box turtles aren't as commonly seen in captivity as the North American box turtles, they are excellent pets nevertheless. Photo of a Yellow-margined Box Turtle, *Cuora flavomarginata*, by Michael Gilroy.

similarity of their common names. I will try to cover as many topics as possible, with the basic goal, if nothing else, of providing the reader with enough useful information to be able to keep these animals alive and well in captivity.

NATURAL HISTORY

The name *Cuora* was first used by Gray back in 1855 although the type species was originally designated *Testudo amboinensis* by Daudin in 1802 (this of course becoming *Cuora amboinensis*, the Southeast Asian Box Turtle, years later). Since that time, nine species have been described, and from those nine a total of four further subspecies make this genus even larger than *Terrapene*.

The range of *Cuora* is, as you might

not those that you can legally acquire), you can keep an adult pair in a glass aquarium as long as the tank is a large one; a 55-gallon would be wonderful although a 30 or a 20 would be passable. The setup would undoubtedly have to be half land and half water, with the water being heated to about 70°F/21°C, and with the faithful inclusion of a full-spectrum light bulb. Since some species are strongly terrestrial, try to keep the land area as dry as possible (it is advised that you learn as much about the natural history of the particular species you have before creating its permanent captive home). Also, since some of the aforementioned terrestrial species also like to bask, it is advised you suspend a small heat lamp just above the land area you have provided.

Remember to clean the tank (i.e., change the water) at least once a week, even if it is filtered. A gravel substrate is good on both the land area and in the water. The photoperiod for these turtles should be about twelve hours per day (six for the full-spectrum bulb, the remaining six with ordinary light) and a moderate amount of humidity should be maintained.

FEEDING

The diet of Asian box turtles seems to vary from species to species, some

MICHAEL GILROY

Most *Cuora* species are eager feeders, but it may take a keeper some time to strike upon what their particular specimen(s) prefer most. Yellow-margined Box Turtle, *Cuora flavomarginata*.

MICHAEL GILROY

Always carefully check over every inch of an Asian box turtle's body before making a purchase. Photo of a Yellow-margined Box Turtle, *Cuora flavomarginata*.

being decidedly herbivorous while others thrive on a diet of raw fish, but the point the keeper should be aware of is that as long as they are given adequate conditions in captivity and

treated well they will take food with great eagerness. The only detail you really have to worry about is offering the right items. The simplest route to take here is to just keep trying different things. Try to make the basic diet varied and include a vitamin supplement at least once every two weeks. Reported foods include the raw fish mentioned above, worms, various fruits and vegetables, some insects, bits of raw meat, and, after a time in captivity, any one of the canned commercial foods, this of course being the easiest, most convenient, and thus most desirable for the enthusiast.

BREEDING

Not too many keepers have bred *Cuora* in captivity, but the process is supposedly much like that of

R. D. BARTLETT

Above: Most of the Asian box turtle species are remarkably attractive. Shown here is a striking Yellow-headed Box Turtle, *Cuora aureocapitata*.
Below: The problem with many of the Asian box turtles is that you may have trouble finding a source from which to get them. Some species are virtually never available. Photo of a Southeast Asian Box Turtle, *Cuora amboinensis*.

MICHAEL GILROY

Above: Hatchling Asian box turtles are often sold and are of course much more preferable than wild-caught specimens. Check all relevant laws, however, before trying to purchase hatchling turtles of any kind. Photo of hatchling Chinese Three-striped Box Turtle, *Cuora trifasciata*.

Below: The Indochinese Box Turtle, *Cuora galbinifrons*, occasionally turns up for sale in the pet trade. It is one of the more terrestrial of the Asian species.

Terrapene, and coaxing them to mate in captivity is apparently not very hard. There have even been reports of male *Cuora* trying to breed with *Terrapene* females, which is certainly most telling.

Apparently a male will bump and

One reason captive-bred *Cuora* turtles are occasionally very expensive is because the mothers only lay two or three eggs each year. Specimen shown is a Yellow-margined Box Turtle, *Cuora flavomarginata*.

MICHAEL GILROY

bite at a female before finally mounting her, then literally clamp himself down onto her carapace, hooking all four claws underneath. After successful copulation, a gestation period of around 60 to 80 days takes place, and finally, in the wild, the eggs are laid in mid-spring to late summer. Notably, egg clutches for these turtles are remarkably small—usually only around two or three. The young are also very small, not usually hatching out at more than 1.6 in/40 mm. They supposedly respond well to captivity and will begin taking soft foods right away. The proper procedures for egg care are basically identical to those of *Terrapene* species.

FURTHER CARE

It is worth noting in conclusion that Asian herptiles of any kind are particularly susceptible to disease during transport. This is usually due to shock and decreased resistance because of the severe change in environment, so be sure to quarantine all specimens for at least a week after acquisition. During this time they should be left alone so they can calm down and get used to their new surroundings. If after this time you suspect a problem, don't try to solve it yourself, but instead bring the animal to a vet immediately. Most box turtle problems can be cured relatively easily if you catch them in their early stages.

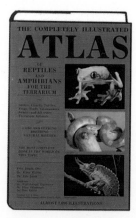

H-1102, 830 pgs, 1800+ photos

TS-165, 655 pgs, (2 vol.), 1800+ photos

PS-876, 384 pgs, 175+ photos

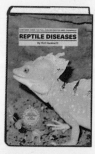

KW-197, 128 pgs, 110+ photos

PS-207, 230 pgs, B&W Illus.

PB-129, 64 pgs, 32 photos

KW-051, 96 pgs, 95 photos

M-515, 64 pgs, 50 B&W photos

CO-026S, 128 pgs, 100 photos

SK-019, 64 pgs, 45 photos

YF-117, 36 pgs, over 20 photos

TT-103, 96 pgs, over 80 photos